Secrets Unearthed, Petals Unfurled

REGINA M BERGEN

To everyone with secrets to keep and secrets to tell—
May they become one and the same.

To those making the same mistakes over and over, expecting
things to turn out differently—
We will make it out of the cycle.

PART ONE

Unearthing Secrets of Myself and Others

~~~

Lightweight

I remember one time, long ago,
I starved myself for almost a year.
I simply didn't eat.
Thin was in, you know?
And, having lost you already,
I was okay with losing myself, too.
I wanted to disappear,
to fade into a vast void,
and cease to exist inside and out.
So, I started to do just that.
As I chipped away at my body,
untaken bite by untaken bite,
run by run, dizzy spells ignored,
I began to vanish from within—
A woman who once was.
I loved that control, that power.
The sickest part of it all, though,
wasn't even about me,
or the idea of intentional starvation,
but how everyone congratulated

me on how fabulous I looked.
How beautiful. How thin. Just stunning!
I must be working so hard!
It never occurred to anyone that
I was slowly withering into nothing.
My mom, guessing the extent I'd gone,
was the only one to tell the truth:
She told me I looked like a bobblehead,
and I should take dieting less seriously.
Only I didn't see it back then,
and neither did anyone else.
Things are different now.
Cancel culture of the heavy
has made me unappealing, undesired.
You'd never know these secrets are mine,
housed in shame within a plus-sized body.
I tell myself that my curves are cool,
"owning them" however I can manage.
But that "thin is in" mantra cuts deep,
and, sometimes, I still wonder exactly
how long I could go without taking a bite.
.... If I really wanted to.

Freedom

There is a deep and profound
comfort in finally finding the strength
to speak your truth out loud,
to offload all of your secrets.
To be free from fear.
Uninhibited.
Unrestrained.
There is power in becoming
unapologetically yourself.
And a unique rush that comes
from simply being you,
while telling the rest of the world
to fuck the fuck right off.

Cool Kids

~~~

Once, when I was younger,
I wanted to be like the cool kids.
So, I went to a party and drank the juice—
Spiked beyond recognition of its starting fruit.
I don't remember much about that night,
except a "friend" throwing some athlete
off a toilet mid-pee, so I could throw up.
I don't think she wanted to clean up a mess.
Then, not wanting to stop her own partying,
she let me pass out in a stranger's bed,
"safe and protected,"
in the arms of some guy I'd heard all about,
but whom I barely actually knew.
I sometimes wonder if he remembers me,
or if he even knew my name at all.
Let's be honest: it's neither here nor there,
I just always wished I could forget his.
And you wonder why I hated high school...

Booze

Whenever I was alone after we were through,
I would sit in my room drowning my sorrows
in cheap vodka - or whatever else I could find
and liberate from my parent's liquor cabinet,
    just to find a way to stop thinking of you.
    It took them a while to notice their bottles
    were out of order and held mostly water.
Or, perhaps, they were merely too frightened
by the person I'd become, my delicate state,
        to bother saying anything about it.
        It was inconsequential, anyway.
I would have gotten it elsewhere, regardless.

    Too old for my age, I had options.

    I remember feeling the sweet rush
      that came with the forgetting—
    A numbness that swept over me,
    like a warm blanket of forgetfulness.

That intoxicating mixture embraced me
like a hug from a long-time friend...
It felt like the only one I had left then.
Remember, I had given them all up for you
under your false pretenses of forever.

We Carry These Things

We carry with us through this life,
all the things we said didn't hurt us,
using them like blocks to construct our walls.
Those impenetrable fortresses of trauma
that we will never admit to building ourselves.
Secrets and lies hiding behind alibis.
We craft barriers to our hearts as we age,
with all the expert precision of a toddler
stealing a cookie from a jar just within reach,
leaving crumbs behind to reveal the truth.
Everyone knows, but nobody tells...
After all, who would be willing to say it aloud?
"Pardon me, but your emotional baggage is showing."

Us

It's been years, and you can
still take my breath away
without even saying a word.
You are the air in my lungs,
toxic, but somehow keeping
me alive and breathing
when my chest feels heavy
with the weight of the world.
One can only carry so much,
before collapsing into self-doubt.
And yet, I hold you still,
grateful for the extra weight
to help keep me grounded,
or maybe drowned.
You're my burden to bear,
heavy and unforgiving of
my minor transgressions,
while you wield an eternal
get-out-of-jail-free card,
created in the image of me.

Granted once in our late 30s,
it stood the test of time,
shielding you from repercussions
for your many indiscretions.
Now, it grows old, just like us,
as we move past forty.
No change in the dynamics
of who we are, what we want,
or where we are going.
Stagnant in this part of our lives,
just like those that came before,
It sometimes seems as if we are
two people fighting a war against
one another, not realizing that
we are both on the same team.
The love is there, but we
just won't let it win.

Charades

∿

Tonight, we're going hard
on sweat, and skin,
and heavy breathing,
while the night looks on,
silently awed by the congruous
form and features that we've
perfected through many years
of being friends with benefits.
Nothing more, nothing less.
Still, somehow, the thought
of ending this charade again
sends fear surging through
the most primitive parts
of my nervous system—
The ones that would make me
do almost anything to avoid
being left alone in a world
without whatever we have—
A world that won't give a fuck
whether or not I live or die,

just barely survive or thrive.
It's all inconsequential.
But, not to me, and not for us.
Thoughts of losing you,
of losing this, are those I
intentionally avoid or ignore,
knowing full well that
a hit of that caliber
would be catastrophic.
It would be my demise...
Especially if I were to let it
take me by surprise—
But, at the same time,
ignorance is bliss,
or so they say.

Gasping

I'm trying to breathe,
but the air isn't coming.
The oxygen here, where I
pass my time, is too thin.
Caught somewhere between
here and there,
alive and dead,
loved and hated,
something and nothing
(It's usually nothing.),
I walk the cobblestone
paths of a life half-lived
in years and experience.
I'm sorry that loving you
is such an inconvenience
to this situationship.
One last gasp,
and I'll find it in me
to take the first step

and finally walk away—
But we both know
that I will be back.

Muse

~~~

I never asked for you to be my muse.
It was a gift, or perhaps a curse,
unwelcomingly bestowed upon me
by too much chemistry, but not
enough truth between us—
A one-sided love met only by
half-hearted attempts at comfort:
"I do care for you."
I know, I know.
It just isn't enough.
I was never enough to
break the walls you built
with your own two hands
after love left you bleeding
once before, in another time.
In another place, with another face.
Maybe someday, someone will
climb those walls, impenetrable to me.
Until then, I'll keep cycling

between loving and hating you,
transforming my pain into
words on a page, as I try,
once again, to walk away from us.

Red Flags

Draw the lines in the sand,
separating the ones who treat
you like you are enough,
from those who never will.
You retreat from the latter,
red flags waving on your horizon,
those you always seem to want,
and pin the former to your wall
as nothing-more-than-friends.
All the while, you cloak your scars
with the smile you keep on reserve,
so you never let them know
how badly they've broken you.
There is so much more to say,
but, like the air when I'm with you,
the words are thin and come
too few and far between.

Predictable

We are nothing
if not predictable.
Two steps forward,
five steps back.
Both running from
the things we are
most afraid of.
The things that
haunt us at night,
as we evade sleep.
We flee from
the possibilities:
You, from love.
Me, from loss.
Both fearing
what tomorrow
could bring,
if we ride this
thing out to
its natural end.

Hearts beneath
our armor,
we push each
other away,
but do you know
how long I've
wanted to tell you
that I love you?

True Colors

Do you recall the first time you lied to me?
—I do—
You talked your way out of it,
—so slick—
Or so you thought, anyway.
—so arrogant—
Your words slithered out from your lips
—like snakes—
Your mouth, still dry and chapped,
—used—
During secret rendezvous with another.
—word venom—
That poisoned us more each time.
—I knew then—
Don't think I didn't always know.
—kept silent—
By the vague shadow of doubt you cast
—your gaslight always burning—
Somehow enough to shut me up.
—temporarily blinded—

Don't think for a moment that I didn't see you
—the real you—
In all of your true colors, a sparkling illusion.
—I saw it all—
But faking it was easier, somehow.
—voluntary blindness—
Chosen over starting all over again
—new place, new person—

I didn't want to start over brand new,
When I'd already put so much time into you.

Nostalgia

Do you remember the time we almost made love
for the first time, drunk at that party
that we never should have been at?
Tangled in someone else's sheets.
Invading someone else's bed.
You stopped it before we got carried away,
saying the timing was all wrong for us—for this.
And it was the first and last time someone
has ever been so kind to me, so caring, so strong.
Strong enough to let me keep what was mine
for just a little bit longer and to save me from myself.
You know I've always been my own worst enemy.
It's no wonder I loved you so deeply and for so long.
I'll never regret you being the first.

Teenage Dating

Blanket down behind the wall in the park,
set flat on the ground in the dark.

Our picnic was crackers and cheese whizz—
and the three beers you stole from your parents.

It really didn't matter, though.
We weren't going to be eating the food.

...But it was the thought that counted.

Traumas

We all have our traumas
that we hide from the light,
woven intricately into each
of the many personas we
carry over our true selves
like a blanket, revealing
only what we allow others to see.
Some hide tiny scars like little secrets,
akin to stolen pennies and lipsticks.
Others hide felony-grade damage
that coats the fibers of our very being,
owning who we are, dictating who we will be,
like a brick pulling us down deeper,
hands tied, drowning us in the past.

Gaslit

It's down deep into the gaslight
that you lose your grip on reality,
just like they'd planned for you.
By then, your sanity has been eradicated,
traded for the lies and manipulation
from the one who promised you forever.

Chances

The moment you realize that
you don't really have a lot left to lose,
is the moment you start taking chances—
And the day you may finally succeed.

Published

Someone asked me today why I had taken
so long to publish my poems.
I stumbled to explain that I couldn't just
put that much of myself onto a page
for others to see, to read, to know.
To read my poems is to plunge
into the deepest trenches of me—all of me:
Who I've been, who I am, who I hope to be.
...And how I got here...
All of the unpretty details,
some downright grotesque.
All the secrets and sacrifices.
To know all of me is to sink entirely in.
Putting it all out there leaves me exposed,
but here I am, finally doing just that.
Even the parts long buried behind a fortress
of selective memory, only revealed by a pen,
in my most private sanctuary for myself alone.
I am ever fearful of being found out, undressed,
and seen for who I really am, with gloves off.

It's like being naked in a room filled with
everyone you've ever known,
an exhibitionist showing off something
private, secret, and so much more than skin deep.
The eyes of others on my poems become
eyes on my heart, my soul, & behind my walls,
so carefully constructed to keep others out.
To invite someone, everyone, into these words
feels like an invasion so deep, so intimate,
that it borders on rape against my very soul.
Lately, though, it feels more consensual.
Still, revealing parts of me to an audience
so potentially violent and volatile, so unknown,
seems akin to sacrificing some part of myself
in the struggle to seek solace in solidarity.
... and that's why it took me so long.

Weak Heart

Stop pining, I tell myself.
He doesn't feel the same.
Let it go, move on, forward march.
One foot in front of the other.
It's not that serious, I say.
So, again, I leave the past behind,
tick another notch into the bedpost
marked 'just not that into me.'
Eternally enough to fuck,
but never enough to love.
Take your friends with benefits
and shove them up your ass.
I add another brick to the wall
I've been building since I was 16,
hoping it will hold, keeping the next
one from getting close enough
that it stings when it winds up
just like all the ones who came before.
Just like every other time.

Bruised

I awoke with a bruise on my shoulder,
and, for a moment, I forgot how it got there.
But visions of your hands on me surface
from somewhere in the depths of my mind,
where I had truly hoped they'd stay.
I'd asked them to remain out of sight,
out of mind—as I'd hoped the bruises would.
I push the memories back, hoping it's the last time.
Maybe this will be the year I can finally disappear.

Not Today

I tell myself I don't need it.
Maybe I don't want it.
But the truth is that I do.
I want, so desperately,
to be taken by surprise
by a love so true, so real
that it makes me realize
every love that came before
was merely for practice.
One that makes me believe
no love will ever come after,
because this is 'the end.'
This is the 'happily ever after.'
Sadly, it hasn't happened today,
and I'm willing to bet it won't tomorrow.

Spark

Don't sell your spark
for a safety net.
In this world of purchase,
you're all you've got.

Walls

There's beauty in the bailout,
when you jump ship to protect
the tattered remains of your heart.
Stack those walls higher next time,
and run a little faster, a little sooner.
Don't let it get so close to love.
You're playing with fire,
and you're going to get burned.

Pause

I hear my brain loud and clear:
Put a pin in those feelings.
Save them for another time,
another place,
another face.

The pause button on my heart
has been sticking as of late,
leading to misplaced
crushes that lead only to
feeling crushed.

Mother

Look for the signs,
they had told me,
when she'd finally passed.
You'll feel her all around you,
see her, find her in nature.
She's still with you.
She will always be with you.
At first, it was a comfort,
until I began to recognize
the cold, hard truth.
Ever a cynic, I roll my eyes,
and scoff at the stupidity,
the absurdity of it all.
She's not here.
If she was, I'd know it.
I'd feel her presence,
know her energy.
She was my world.
Trust me, I'd know.
Truth bomb?

SECRETS UNEARTHED, PETALS UNFURLED

I'm glad she's not here.
If she were watching all this,
witnessing my days unfolding,
she would see exactly
how my life worked out...
and it would kill her
(if she wasn't already dead).
I'm sorry, Mom.
I really am trying.

Issues

I went to therapy for a while
to get my head straight
after my life fell apart.
But, as always, I was more
concerned about the praise
than the actual healing.
I'm a people pleaser to the core.
The eternal good girl,
whatever that means
to whoever I'm pleasing.
By the time I stopped going,
I had her convinced I would
make something great of myself,
despite the shreds that he left behind.
I was her favorite success story,
fully healed after just a couple of months.
Now, if only I'd told her the truth...
I'd probably have been hospitalized.

Sleep

I used to sleep next to a man.
I wore that ring for 11 years,
but we still never knew each other.
Now, I share my bed with 3 dogs.
And, if I'm being honest,
there isn't much that I miss from before.
Maybe next time will be better.

Insomnia

Every night for two weeks,
I've woken up at 4 am, inexplicably,
and written several poems
before falling back to sleep.
It's as if the words are forcing
my eyes open just long enough
to put them down on paper,
begging me to release them
from their cage in a last-ditch effort
to repair my heart & comfort my chaos,
before I start to lose my mind.
Is this healing or insanity?

Somethings

I'll always want the ones who don't want me back—
Not really, anyway. Not enough. Not even close.
A fatal flaw, forcing me into eternal statuses of
"casual" and "friends with benefits,"
when I want so much more than that.
I guess I've just been taking what I can get.
Something is better than nothing, right?
Even if it hurts like hell to know you're still
out there looking for more when I'm right here
with your arms wrapped around me,
full weekends at a time, sometimes.
Waiting. Hoping. Holding my breath.
Someday, you'll see me here... really see me.
It's just not going to be today or tomorrow.

Hate

I told him I hated him today.
My censor stopped working, I guess.
It slipped out from the depths of my hurt,
kept hidden for so long, secret and safe,
into the world like a thief in the night.
I hated who he was and would always be,
the way he made me feel powerless.
I hated that I kept coming back
to the endless cycle of bliss, then regret,
trapped by forces I still hadn't learned
to overcome by strength or willpower.
Tethered to self-sabotage by desire,
my inability to choose to love someone
who had it in them to love me back.
I told him in the throngs of passion
just how much I hated him,
and he thought that it was hot...
Just another red flag to add to the list.

Ghosted

Driving, taking the long way,
I have time to think...
A dangerous act for one
so prone to overthinking.
My mind jumps around,
unable to focus on anything—
Except for what I'm trying to forget.
Turn it off, I plead silently.
Make the flood of thoughts vanish,
just as he did, without a trace.
Now, he is just another ghost
haunting my heart and my head,
hunting for what's left of me—
To have, to hold, to leave me cold.

Fake

~~~

I bend.
I break.
I fold.
I fake.
Anything
To
Make
You
Believe
Am
Who
You
Want
Me
To
Be.

The Things I Want

What I want from you
is for you not to walk away
as I end this situationship
in search of something more—
To realize that maybe I'm worth keeping.
Perhaps having and holding,
even if it forces you to become
A one-woman man, how tragic!
Your biggest fear in life, realized.
I want to feel like I was more than
just another quarter-hearted fling,
more than a romp in the hay
or a notch in your bedpost.
You don't. You can't. You won't.
So, I walk away once again,
knowing it's only a matter of time
before I come running back.
Just like precise clockwork,
the ticking hands of this cycle

will begin anew, sparking passion
along with soul-crushing toxicity.
 You were the only one I wanted,
but sometimes that's not enough.

Lost

Where do you go when your
heart starts to wonder if
this is even worth it anymore?
Year after year of searching
passes by in the blink of an eye.
Seeking but never finding
something, anything,
that burns with the tiniest spark,
the possibility of becoming
something real, something pure.
You tell yourself to hold on.
Be patient, be positive, be true.
Stay kind, stay good, stay you.
It's all coming down the pike.
...Just wait for the flame to ignite...
Still, I can't help but wonder
if we've used up all the magic
this world had to offer, and now,
we are stuck behind the bars
of this mundane trap of existence

with no chance of escape.
Have we lost the ability to
create love that conquers all?
Or, at the very least, that lasts
longer than a one-or-two-night stand?
Or is this just a me thing?

Trap

You make me feel like
no more than a small animal
caught in a sticky glue trap.
Struggling, spitting, hissing.
Your words tempt me, bait me—
And I run to you, just like every time,
knowing full well that it will destroy me.
But, this time, I'll chew my limbs off
before I let myself think that I'm yours.

Narcissist

I try not to blame myself for the
way things worked out between us.
But, if not me, then who?
Surely, not you. Never you.
Despite the undeniable truth
that you took to the flint,
lighting the gaslight like a torch,
with every fiber of your being,
until it became your whole persona.
And you had me thinking it was me!
Me, all along, who caused the cuts.
Me, who sliced those deep rifts
into all that we once were,
bleeding it out until it lay silent,
motionless on the floor of the house
that we once called our home.

Security

This is how we'll do it,
to stay safe and sound
in these treacherous times
when hearts break like
shattering crystal glasses
dropped from table to floor,
nary a care for their survival.
Love is a cocktail reception
torn asunder until it becomes
a wake - solemn and sad.
I don the burial shroud,
but I wear it oh-so-well.
So, here is the plan, then:
You protect your own heart,
and I'll safeguard mine,
with thick bubble wrap—
-No-
Something stronger.
Steel.

-No, stronger-
Hydrocarbon body armor?
Excellent
We take no chances here.
No one gets in to ensure
that no one will try to get out.
Not now. Not again. No thanks.
I can't handle another goodbye.
Another MIA:
Missing
In
Amour.
Another UFO:
Unexplained
Fleeting
Object of my affection.
"But how will you find love
if you don't let anyone in?"
they ask again and again.
And the answer is simple:
When the stars align,
and the time is right,
'the one' will come bearing
weaponry of words that
leave me defenseless,
yearning for things I fear.
My walls will crumble
and I will wonder what
right I ever had to refuse
to let love in easily when it
sought entry into this fortress.
And...if he never arrives,
if he isn't strong enough to

SECRETS UNEARTHED, PETALS UNFURLED

to reach me over my
high walls, deep moats,
and damage masked as dragons,
then, oh well...
At least I still have my dogs.

Excuses

"When do you sleep?" he asked,
and I chuckle, despite the stark,
cold, seriousness in his tone.
I know where this is headed already.
"I don't, really," I say dully, flatly,
prepared for the return argument,
awaiting the refusal to believe
I could get by on so little rest.
It's not like I enjoy it; it simply is.
"You must be exaggerating."
A statement greeted by my
trademarked eye roll and shrug.
No use discussing it further.
He won't understand, anyway.
He's not of the same ilk,
for his mind comes with the
standard on/off switch mine lacks.
This is the perfect excuse for why
we would never, could never,
and should never work out.

Another reason to remain alone.
So, I pack up my heart again,
and pull the drawstrings tight,
closing it up to head for the hills.
Today seems like the perfect
day to disappear without a trace.

Secrets

I've revealed so many of my secrets lately,
that I find myself scraping the bottom
of the barrel, searching for the sweet
taste of the freedom and release
that comes with shoving them out into
the world without fear, without shame.
Only now, the secrets grow darker.
Those left are the ones buried deep,
housed in the dark recesses of memory,
shackled to the walls behind a thick
curtain of iron bars and false promises.
They're heavily guarded, deep in the psyche,
by those who once pledged to do no harm,
but whose whispers still haunt me
in the sleeping and waking hours alike.
And, slumber evades me even more now
than it did back then, when it was all fresh.
These are the stories that were never
meant to see the light of day.
Too dangerous. Too destructive.

SECRETS UNEARTHED, PETALS UNFURLED

The ones I still can't bring myself
to speak or write back into this world,
for fear of setting them free from their dungeons.
I fear the backlash from the all-too-real dragons
that guard them with firey tongues,
still burning terror into the depths of my soul,
even after all these years of growing up.
So, your secrets, my secrets, will be kept
under lock and key, protected by memory alone,
like an assassin that refuses to let me move on.
You will continue to have my silence,
winning, once again, but let's be real:
You always knew that you would
come out of this with the upper hand.
After all, you cut my tongue out with trauma
when I was still only just a child.

Kneeling

I can smile through almost anything.
Haven't you learned that about me yet?
You will never, ever get the satisfaction
of knowing your words have the power
to bring me to my knees in agony,
begging for the strength to carry on.

Here's the Thing

~∽∽~

The thing about me is that I'm
one of the most open people
you will meet in this world.
Now, anyway. It wasn't always so.
I learned long ago that the parts
I most want to hide are the ones
that make people trust me.
I don't keep who I am hidden.
Not now. Not anymore.
I'm an open book—high reading level.
I'm out there on display every day,
deep flaws and all, because it's all me.
I am irreparably awkward,
a trait only recently embraced.
My life is chaos—sheer, utter absurdity.
My world has been turned upside down
more times than I could ever count,
and I'm still trying to upright it.
I'm flat broke all the time, always.
Just trying to stay afloat, fighting waves,

but usually sinking in the process.
But I haven't drowned quite yet.
Side hustles, selling things, searching
for quarters between couch cushions.
It's a daily struggle to overcome the
incessant doom bagging—all the things.
All the things, all the time.
And I often fail, letting clutter invade!
I'm not a very good friend, either.
Too unreliable—and I disappear.
A big regret in my life thus far.
I hyper-focus on certain things,
abandoning others, including friendships,
and sometimes even family.
And I don't notice it until it is too late,
too long ignored to make amends.
I have social anxiety, hate crowds, and
I always feel like everyone is looking at me,
judging me, finding new things to mock.
My weight, my clothes, my walk, whatever.
I will never like myself physically,
but, a well-aimed selfie with
good lighting and the right makeup
can make all the fat seem less... fat.
There's a lot more to tell, but far too
much for a poem that's already jumping
all over the place with no attention
to form, only to function.
Ladies and gentlemen... welcome!
It's all a shit show, but it's my shit show.

You

Your words—dangerous words
that can both hurt and heal.
Are they torpedoes or triage today?
Enough to leave me breathless,
lost in the sea of your eyes.
They could be used to craft
a love so deep it could conquer
even the toughest of obstacles.
Or they could crumble bridges
and burn them to the ground
as you walk away from me
without a backward glance.
So, what's it going to be this time?

Hate to Love You

When the words, "I hate you,"
sliced my lips apart as
we held each other close,
it was unexpected, unintended.
They came without a warning,
oozing out like blood after
a well-placed fist to the mouth.
You knew what they really meant,
without me saying anything else.
It was a code you understood,
but neither of us could admit
that the venom spewed with callous
disregard for the truth was a crutch,
a mere placeholder for the true feelings
I could never allow to escape
the confines of my fragile heart
and into the light of day.
How could I ever begin to explain
that "I hate you" translated roughly
into "I love you, but you're breaking my heart?"

It's in the Leaving

～～

When the pining all gets old and
filling the void seems less essential
than safeguarding your sanity,
it's time to walk away again.
To leave behind the 'maybes'
and 'what ifs' for the sure thing,
for the structurally sound,
for the long walk off the short cliff,
and into the safety net so carefully
crafted during the trauma years.
The same one that will eventually
become your burial shroud
when they put you in the dirt alone,
with no one present to mourn
the loss of their one-and-only.

Self-preservation is nowhere when you're
standing still, frozen, trapped here.
It's found only in the abrupt turn-and-run,

the escape from what could have been,
and the return to what was, what is,
and what you will always go back to.
It's in the leaving that you are protected.
You'll never be the one left behind.
Not ever again. Lesson learned.
(In the hardest way possible, as always.)
So, despite the sting, you go, you leave,
knowing full well that the first step
is always the hardest, but that
the first cut will remain the deepest.
That's a scar that will never disappear.
This time will pale in comparison,
and that knowledge gives you strength.

Fingers cold on the light switch,
you take one final glance behind
to make sure you haven't forgotten
anything (besides your whole world.)
One foot in front of the other,
feet fall heavy on the hardwood,
as the door slam echoes through the
space that was never really yours.
This was merely temporary housing
for a heart worn down to almost nothing,
threadbare, thin, battered, and bruised.
It's in the leaving that you find tomorrow,
whether it's for better or for worse,
just like you always knew you would.
This was never going to be forever.
And, starting life over again,
...Again...
You swear next time will be different,

that next time maybe you'll stay.
...But you won't...
It's in the leaving and the loss
that you will always be found.

The First Letters

~~~

Fooled by your toxic smile,
Under your spell I fall.
Couldn't you have granted me the
Kindness of staying away?

You only come back
Once I begin to heal; and always
Under false pretenses...

Not this time.
Do you get the message?

Urban Musing

I thought about it today,
while passing through the
rougher parts of a city
known for its violent crime.
Traveling in connection with
a job that remains necessary,
but a detour from my dreams,
I entered the inner-city streets,
a slave to my GPS and the
unbiased directions it speaks.
I sank down in my seat,
closed the car windows,
and clicked the lock button,
trying to avoid taking up
any obvious space in this
world where I don't belong.
Attempting to fit in when
too much of my innocence
remains intact and unscathed,
having only faced what boils

down to a bevy of first-world,
sad, white-girl problems,
mostly of my own making.
(I'm not racist, but I can
recognize when I've had it easy).
I see the senseless inequality.
As the streets grew wider,
and the structures shifted
to familiar suburban sprawl,
I felt comforted and safe again.
No longer an outsider invading
this place that isn't mine...
Until it occurred to me that
all the pretty, white fences, new SUVs,
and tree-lined streets with
Little Free Libraries on every corner,
all the luxuries in the whole world
won't save anyone, anywhere
once their time has come.
So, I go about my hustle,
thankful for such brief moments
of clarity in my otherwise
cloudy consciousness.

Unappreciated

I'm so tired of being the angel,
the saint, the one who bends
over backward for everyone
else to make sure they're okay.

When does it start to matter
whether I'm alright or not?
When do I stop rolling over
and submitting to others?

I've had enough of being the
Queen of Kindness or the
Goddess of Goodness.
It's time to be selfish, for once.

This time, I am saving myself
before anyone else because
it's abundantly clear that
no one is rescuing me in return.

Okay

When I said we should stop
seeing each other like this—
the way we were,
the things we did—
I didn't expect your
response to simply be:
"Okay."
I thought there would be
a brief debate or
a conversation, at least.
I guess I probably
should have known better.
It's not like it was our
first time down this road.
When I questioned it,
and you only responded,
"I don't want to fight,"
all I could think of was...
After all we've done,
after all we've shared,

told one another
under cover of night
and blankets,
I'm not even worth a fight.
Then again, it's you.
You collect "I love you's"
like trophies, then run.

PART TWO

Petals Unfurled: Earth Verses

The Sky

The sky is strange today—
Faded yellow, blue, and gray,
like a bruise, like the past.
The wind picks up quickly,
tossing dead pine needles
against the living room window
as I sit, lost somewhere between
writing and staring at the walls,
frozen in the struggle between
all the things I want to do
and the things I have to do.
So, rather than fight the battle,
I do nothing, and nothing gets done.
Still, I can't help but notice the sky,
accusatory and angry,
like a bruise. Like the past.

Springtime Renewal

Readying itself for the warmth of the sun,
Earth awakens,
rubbing its sleepy eyes, to see that another
winter has passed,
leaving cool rains to replace the icy,
seemingly endless grip of winter.

There's magic in the springtime
that can't be found anywhere else.
Deep petrichor triggers the senses to awaken
and bear witness to it—
To the re-awakening of the Earth,
arising from a frosty slumber.

It stretches its limbs as the rain
melts the frozen ground, puddling.
Refusing to stay down, Earth shakes itself off,
spraying water in all directions.
Rising to its feet, the planet welcomes
the incoming season with open arms.

SECRETS UNEARTHED, PETALS UNFURLED

Preparing to pop seeds, long set
beneath the dirt, into seedlings,
readying itself to embrace longer days and warmer soil,
Earth pours the promise of tomorrow out
with the rains of early spring.

It chants: We made it. We have survived.
Now, we must grow.
Not a bad lesson to learn with the coming of a new season.

If Earth Could Speak

The sky above threatens with menacing grumbles.
Lightning flashes, sharp, from angry, tear-streaked eyes,
while Earth shouts booming battle cries, it secretly sobs:
"Back off. Leave me be. I didn't want any of this!"
We brought this upon ourselves, though;
now there's no going back.
Angry over years of neglect and downright abuse
at the hands of humanity,
Earth urges those who would fight against
the power of nature to flee,
to back the fuck down and crawl away,
tail between their legs.
Lowly humans, you're nothing for the
power and strength of this Earth.
Will you never learn the lessons from the ones
who came before?
The majestic, interwoven powers-that-be are
ancient and omnipotent.
They know things you can't hope
to grasp or understand in your lifetime—

And yet you worship the false idols
of technology, wealth, and power,
throwing away the beauty
of balance, nature, unity, and interconnectedness.
You have no one to blame but yourselves
for the outcome of your choices,
and with that, I bid you adieu and wish you the best...
Always remember that in the end,
Earth will win—and you will perish.
This has all happened before. It will happen again.
Nothing good comes from ignoring the lessons
you should have learned long ago.

The Dance of the Butterfly

Butterflies don't merely fly,or flap, or flutter.
They dance.
They rise and fall with the wind,
moving in chaotic, joyous splendor.
Wings splashed in color paint the sky
as they select the perfect Earthly firework.
They perch upon flowers on long, thin legs,
probing for nectar to power them through
their ongoing flight from bloom to bloom.
They dance as if the world isn't watching—
And for the most part, it isn't.
We've long ago lost the desire to truly see,
our eyes closed to the splendor around us.
We could learn a few tricks from them—
The merengue of the monarchs.
The frolicking of the fritillaries.
The sashaying of the swallowtails.
We could learn to dance for ourselves,
living like there is no tomorrow.

We could be so much better
than what we've become.

Not Today

If you sit quietly outside, surrounded by nature,
you can hear the bees, the birds, and
the cicadas screaming in their trees.
Is it a scream of sorrow or a cry of joy?
You can feel the wind as it moves branches,
while the sun shines, warming your skin—
Then, out of nowhere, a bug flies into your ear.

Ew. Nevermind. I'm going inside.

Garden Song

The butterflies and bumblebees flit
from flower to flower—
First the yellow, then the purple—
Searching for the perfect bloom.

They dance together in the breeze
as wind chimes play a melody.
Sometimes you forget to hear them,
but if you listen, the song is always there.

Reminders

On days like today, I try to force my mind to go blank,
but it always returns to the hustle and bustle—
The stress of all the things I haven't done,
and the chaos of an ever-lengthening list of "shoulds."
If I find a few moments to try to forget,
I know I'll be better able to face the day.
So, I sit by the garden that I built from the ground up—
Where my mother's memory is encased
in every square foot.
Every plant. Every flower. Every statue.
Every painted rock.
It's the place where the breeze whispers in her voice,
a spirit guiding me, telling me that everything is okay—
That I can make it through, and this, too, shall pass.
The wasps, bees, and spiders no longer frighten me
the way they once did for so long during childhood.
Now, I understand the power of systems and connections.
They are all a part of this interconnected web, this beauty.
And, only together, can they form
the perfection before me.

SECRETS UNEARTHED, PETALS UNFURLED

They play their roles and perform their duties,
just like I do.
Just as we all do, even when we're almost ready to quit.
I come here to forget about the chaos
and remember the calm.
I gave myself an hour to sit outside today,
the garden all around me—
To let it work its magic. To center me. To ground me.
I pulled up a chair and placed it beside the garden border,
and I can feel my skin burning in the light of the sun—
But I don't care as the breeze
whispers its magic into my ears,
working some primal therapeutic peace
into my mind and my body.
Even the buzzing of a fly near my ear
no longer bothers me,
for I'm not an outsider, but part of the system,
part of the Earth.
For a time, I am a fully immersed piece
of a primeval natural magic—
One that has kept this planet going long before
humanity befell her.
This is my time to remember that
just because the world feels crazy,
there's still tranquility to be found
if you know where to search,
and, realistically, most things I'm concerned about
don't matter—
They are mere drops in the bucket: Teeny. Tiny. Trivial.
First-world human problems that mean nothing
on a grander scale.
Universally unimportant.

Sunburn

Today, I let myself get a sunburn.
I asked for it, in fact—begged.
I sat outside in the garden,
watching the bumblebees
and the butterflies
jump from plant to plant.
Dragonflies darted around in circles.
Even a hummingbird hovered
from flower to flower seeking nectar.
I let the sun's rays beat down on my skin,
to remind me that I'm human,
and still part of this Earth,
not above its power and flex.
I have no control—none.
Pretending merely leads to demise.
So, I sat outside in the sun,
and I let it all go for once.
I let the sun hit my skin,
drawing sweat from my pores.
I let the sweet breeze tickle my ears

and push my hair from my face.
I was as I was meant to exist—
Without protection. Vulnerable.
Did I want to know the pain? No.
I merely wanted to recall
what it's like to feel something real,
beyond the stress and overwhelm—
And embrace my powerlessness over nature.
My life is merely a drop in the universal bucket,
and whether I fail or succeed is trivial
to all but me and those who love me.
Today, I let myself get a sunburn,
to remember how something real feels,
to prove that I am still of this Earth.

About the Author

Regina Bergen lives with her three children and two rescue dogs in the beautiful Hudson Valley region of New York. She has a B.A. in Environmental Studies and Latin American Studies and a Master's in Public Administration from Pace University.

Before writing and editing full-time, Regina worked as a fundraiser at a global environmental conservation organization and spent several years as a stay-at-home mom. She loves the outdoors, animals, cooking, coffee, and spending her free time with her kids and pets.

Social Media – Get in Touch!
Facebook, TikTok, Instagram,
and Goodreads: ReginaBergenAuthor

www.ReginaBergen.com

WritingbyRegina@gmail.com